WOW! Wildlife

Amazing
Animals at Night

by Alix Wood

WINDMILL BOOKS
New York

Published in 2013 by Windmill Books,
An Imprint of Rosen Publishing
29 East 21st Street, New York, NY 10010

Editor for Alix Wood Books: Mark Sachner
US Editor: Sara Antill
Designer: Alix Wood
Consultant: Sally Morgan

Photo Credits: Cover, 1, 2, 3, 4, 5, 6, 7, 8, 9, 10, 11 (bottom left and bottom right), 12, 13 (top), 14, 15
(bottom), 16, 17, 18, 19, 20 (top), 21, 22, 23 © Shutterstock; 11 (top) © Luciano Leone; 13 (middle and
bottom) © iStock; 15 (top) © Una Smith; 20 (bottom) © Francesco Costa

Library of Congress Cataloging-in-Publication Data

Wood, Alix.
 Amazing animals at night / by Alix Wood.
     p. cm. — (Wow! wildlife)
 Includes index.
 ISBN 978-1-4488-8102-4 (library binding) — ISBN 978-1-4488-8165-9 (pbk.) —
ISBN 978-1-4488-8173-4 (6-pack)
 1. Nocturnal animals—Juvenile literature. I. Title.
 QL755.5.W66 2013
 591.5'18—dc23

                                    2012007003

Manufactured in the United States of America

CPSIA Compliance Information: Batch #B1S12WM: For Further Information contact Windmill Books, New York, New York at 1-866-478-0556

Contents

What Does Nocturnal Mean?

After you go to bed at night, many animals are just waking up. Animals that are most active at night are called **nocturnal**. Nocturnal animals like the dark for different reasons. Some use darkness to hide from danger. Others like nighttime because it is cooler than daytime or because it is easier to find food at night.

This leopard is a great nighttime hunter. With good eyesight, sharp hearing, and soft footsteps, it can creep up on its **prey** in the dark and then pounce.

Nocturnal animals have clever ways to get around at night. They often have at least one sense that is very strong—sight, hearing, touch, taste, or smell.

Bat-eared foxes' big ears help them find food. They can even hear an animal moving around underground!

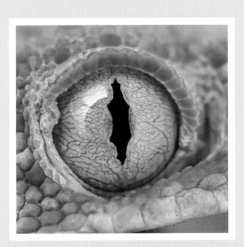

WOW! Night Vision

This tokay gecko eye has a very narrow pupil in daylight. The pupil is the dark area in the middle of the eye. At night, the pupil gets bigger and fills most of the eye. This lets in more light so the gecko can see better. Geckos see only in black and white. At night they don't need to see in color. The tokay gecko also changes its own skin color at night to help hide itself! It is dark gray with orange-red spots in the daytime, and light gray with bluish spots in the dark.

Getting Away from the Heat

In hot places, many animals are nocturnal. They only come out when it is cooler, at night. Many animals sleep under a tree or in a cool den, cave, or **burrow** in the heat of the day.

In Australia, wombats (right) live in burrows, away from the heat of the day. They come out at night to feed. Wombats have poor eyesight and rely on their great sense of smell to find food in the dark. Their strength and speed earned them the nickname "bulldozers of the bush," as they run straight through things in their path, including any fences!

These lions are taking it easy in the heat of the African sun. They hunt for food at dawn and dusk, when it is cooler. Females do most of the hunting.

Vipers hide in the dark and wait for their prey. They can tell from ground vibrations if an animal is close or if it is too large for them to eat. Vipers strike and then follow the **scent** of their **poisoned** prey in the darkness.

A pit viper hunting at night.

WOW! Check Your Shoes!

Scorpions stay hidden away from the hot sun. They like to hide in snug spaces. If a scorpion hides in a house, it will often hide in shoes! Some scorpions have poison strong enough to kill a person.

Hunting in the Dark

For many **predators**, the best time to hunt is at night. The darkness hides them so they can easily sneak up on prey. Many big cats are nocturnal. The cougar pictured below is both nocturnal and **crepuscular**. "Crepuscular" means active at dawn and dusk.

WOW! Big Cat!

Cougars (also called pumas or mountain lions) live in North America and South America. They have large paws and strong back legs. They stalk their prey and then leap onto its back. A cougar can leap as high as 18 feet (5.4 m)!

Hunting at night means less competition for food. Other hunters are asleep, so you have a better chance of finding a good meal.

Owls eat snakes and **rodents**. There are plenty of snakes out at night, hunting for food. This grass snake (right) hunts near water and likes to eat toads and frogs, which also come out at night. The natterjack toad (below) eats insects and even small snakes.

Many nocturnal animals hunt other animals that are nocturnal. It's almost as if there is a day shift and a night shift of hunters and hunted! Plenty of prey are active at night, so most hunters will not go hungry.

Hiding in the Dark

A good reason for only coming out at night is that you are more likely to be seen and hunted during the day. The shadows of the night can keep you hidden.

Snails are nocturnal for two good reasons. They don't want to dry up, and they don't want to be eaten by birds and other daytime predators. Snails hide during the day under leaves and stones. They eat plants, so they can get a meal at any time of day.

Snails in Europe have to watch out for the hedgehog (below). It loves to eat snails and is nocturnal, too.

If the dark doesn't hide hedgehogs well enough from their predators, they can always curl up in a ball. Their sharp spines stick out and protect them. Only badgers are strong enough to uncurl them!

Predators will often hunt by sensing movement in the dark. If an animal can stay still, the predator may go away. The tapeti is a type of rabbit from Brazil, in South America. It can keep totally still for over 10 minutes!

The tapeti has been known to swim away from danger. It's the only type of rabbit that can swim.

WOW! Hiding in the Daytime?

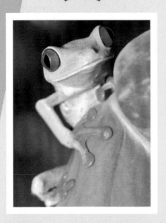

The nocturnal red-eyed tree frog has a problem. How do you hide in the daytime if you are this bright? Simple. Shut your bright red eyes and sit on your bright orange feet!

Super Sense: Smell and Taste

A good sense of smell is important to many nocturnal animals for finding food, sensing danger, and finding a mate. Many animals also use **scent marking** to mark their territory. A scent mark will stay as a warning long after the animal that made it has left. It's a little like putting up a "Keep Out" sign!

Wolves hold their heads high to sniff the air. Their long snouts hold millions of scent receptors. Their sense of smell is about 100 times better than ours. In the right weather, wolves can smell their prey from about 1.75 miles (2.8 km) away!

Snakes use their forked tongues to taste and smell the world. The faster they flick, the more they are sniffing! Tongues take the smell and taste to a special part on the roof of their mouths. The fork in the tongue helps them sense the direction the smell comes from.

Some snakes also have a special **groove** in their heads that acts like a heat sensor. It tells them where prey is by sensing their body heat.

Pangolins (left) use their great sense of smell at night to find insects. They can roll up in a scaly ball if there is danger. They squirt a smelly liquid from their rear if anyone tries to unroll them!

WOW! A Bird with a Nose

Birds generally have little or no sense of smell. Kiwis, from New Zealand, though, have **nostrils** at the end of their beaks. They can find worms by smell when they probe the soil at night.

Super Sense: Sight

Sight is still a very important sense for animals at night. Many animals have special eyes to help them see in the darkness.

Tarsiers have enormous eyes to help them see at night. Each eye is bigger than the animal's brain! Tarsiers have excellent hearing and can fold and unfold their big funnel-like ears. They catch their prey by jumping at it. They eat insects, birds, snakes, lizards, and bats.

Tarsier's eyes are so big they can't move them to look around. They have to turn their head!

Cats' eyes are only slightly smaller than human eyes. But a cat can open its pupil (the black area in the middle) three times wider than humans can. This means more light can enter the eye and seeing in the dark is easier.

Shiny Eyes

Many nocturnal animals' eyes glow when light shines into them. Their eyes have a mirrorlike back that reflects the light. The color they shine depends on the animal. Rats' eyes shine red, raccoons' eyes shine yellow, and horses' eyes shine blue!

This baby owl's forward-facing eyes are perfect for night hunting. Using two eyes at once makes judging distances easier. An owl can turn its head almost all the way around to see behind! It can't see well close up, though.

Super Sense: Touch

We can feel our way with our hands in the dark, but most of us are not very good at it! Many nocturnal animals have an amazing sense of touch that helps them get around in the darkness.

Whiskers are a great way for animals to feel their way around in the dark. Big cats hold their whiskers out to the side when hunting to sense the slightest movement. When they have pounced, they pull their whiskers forward like a net around their prey, so they can feel if it tries to escape.

Even in daytime, rats rely more on their whiskers than their eyes to find their way around. When this young rat's whiskers touch something, they bend, and send an image of the object to the rat's brain.

WOW! Owls Have Whiskers, Too

Owls can't see well close up, but they can feel their prey with special feathers around their feet and beak when they are close. The hairlike feathers around the beak help the owl find prey it may have dropped and can't see.

Raccoons have very sensitive fingers that they use to find frogs and crayfish under stones in the water at night. Raccoons also have whisker-like hairs on the tips of their fingers to help their sense of touch. Raccoons often wash their food. Wetting their paws makes their sense of touch work better. Raccoons have very nimble fingers on their front feet and can untie knots, turn doorknobs, and even open jars!

A raccoon fishing in a stream, feeling under stones for crayfish

Super Sense: Hearing

Having sharp hearing and being able to move around silently are both useful skills in the dark.

Big ears are a clue that this serval (right) has good hearing. A serval has very long legs that help it keep its head above the grass as it hunts. A serval will listen for the smallest movements and then it will pounce on its prey.

Servals can even hear prey moving underground!

Bats have an amazing super sense to find their way in the dark, called **echolocation**. Bats make a sound that is too high-pitched for us to hear. This sound bounces off objects and makes an echo, which bats use to map their surroundings.

Slow lorises move slowly and deliberately. They make little or no noise as they move. When danger is near, they stay completely still and silent.

WOW! ## Softly, Softly

Most flying birds make a noise as air rushes over the wing. An owl's wing has a comblike feather edge that muffles the noise and allows the owl to fly silently. This lets the owl hear and then capture potential prey.

Glowing in the Dark

When it's dark, it's a good idea to carry your own flashlight! Some creatures can light up the dark with their own bodies.

Many sea creatures living in the dark depths of the oceans glow in the dark. Why? Amazingly, the glow makes it harder to see them. From below, their glow blends in with the dim light coming from the surface. This jellyfish uses light to hide!

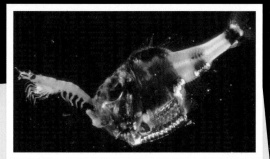

WOW! Hatchetfish

This strange see-through fish is a marine hatchetfish. It has just caught a snack! Like most deep-sea fish, its very sensitive eyes point upward looking for prey against the light. Like the jellyfish, it creates its own lights, which point downward, to disguise itself.

The firefly (right) is actually a winged beetle. In its **larva** state, the firefly is commonly known as a glow worm. Fireflies produce a substance that creates light when it mixes with air. They glow to attract a mate and to avoid predators. A firefly's glow is made from a nasty-tasting substance, and after a predator eats one, it quickly learns not to do it again!

Want to find a scorpion in the dark? Take a UV or black light with you, and scorpions will glow blue-green. No one is too sure why this happens. It could be that their glowing outer covering helps them sense light, kind of like a giant eyeball glowing in the dark!

Glossary

burrows (BUR-ohz)
Holes in the ground made by animals for shelter or protection.

crepuscular (creh-PUS-kyu-ler)
Active during twilight.

echolocation
(eh-koh-loh-KAY-shun)
A way of locating objects by making sound waves that bounce off the objects and back to the sender.

groove (GROOV)
A long narrow channel made in a surface.

larvae (singular *larva*)
(LAHR-vee)
The young wormlike stage of many insects after they hatch from the egg.

nocturnal (nok-TUR-nul)
Active at night.

nostrils (NOS-trulz)
The outer openings of the nose through which one breathes.

poisoned (POY-zund)
Killed or injured by a harmful substance.

predators (PREH-duh-terz)
Animals that live by killing
and eating other animals.

prey (PRAY)
An animal hunted or killed
by another animal for food.

scent (SENT)
An odor left by an animal.

scent markings
(SENT MAR-kingz)
An odor left by an animal, often
by urinating, which acts as a
signal to other animals.

rodents (ROH-dents)
Small mammals, for example
mice, squirrels, or beavers, that
have sharp front teeth used for
gnawing.

Websites

For web resources related to the
subject of this book, go to:
www.windmillbooks.com/weblinks
and select this book's title.

Read More

Clark, Ginjer C. *Black Out!: Animals that Live in the Dark*. All Aboard Science Reader. New York: Grosset & Dunlap, 2008.

Kalman, Bobbie. *Night Animals*. My World. New York: Crabtree Publishing, 2011.

Mattern, Joanne. *Bats Are Night Animals*. Night Animals. New York: Gareth Stevens, 2007.

Index